GREAT MINDS OF SCIENCE

MARIE CURIE

Physics and Chemistry Pioneer

by Katherine Krieg

Content Consultant
Peter Soppelsa, PhD
Assistant Professor, History of Science
University of Oklahoma

Core Library

An Imprint of Abdo Publishing
www.abdopublishing.com

www.abdopublishing.com

Published by Abdo Publishing, a division of ABDO, PO Box 398166, Minneapolis, Minnesota 55439. Copyright © 2015 by Abdo Consulting Group, Inc. International copyrights reserved in all countries. No part of this book may be reproduced in any form without written permission from the publisher. Core Library™ is a trademark and logo of Abdo Publishing.

Printed in the United States of America, North Mankato, Minnesota
042014
092014

Cover Photo: Bettmann/Corbis/AP Images
Interior Photos: Bettmann/Corbis/AP Images, 1, 4, 17, 20, 28, 37, 43, 45; Shutterstock Images, 6, 15; Bridgeman Art, 9, 12; Library of Congress/Corbis, 19; Underwood & Underwood/Corbis, 24; Red Line Editorial, 26, 39; Lebrecht Music & Arts/Corbis, 32; Library of Congress, 34

Editor: Jenna Gleisner
Series Designer: Becky Daum

Library of Congress Control Number: 2014932589

Cataloging-in-Publication Data
Krieg, Katherine.
 Marie Curie: physics and chemistry pioneer / Katherine Krieg.
   p. cm. -- (Great minds of science)
Includes bibliographical references and index.
ISBN 978-1-62403-377-3
1. Curie, Marie, 1867-1934--Juvenile literature. 2. Chemists--France--Biography--Juvenile literature. 3. Women chemists--France--Biography--Juvenile literature. I. Title.
540.92--dc23
[B]
                                                          2014932589

CONTENTS

CHAPTER ONE

POLISH PRIDE

In a time when men ruled the science world, Marie Curie stood alone as a female scientist. Today, she stands out in history as the first woman to win a Nobel Prize. She is also the only person to win two Nobel Prizes in two different sciences: physics in 1903 and chemistry in 1911. Even in the face of adversity, Curie would manage to impact the world with her scientific discoveries.

To this day, Marie Curie is the only person to ever win a Nobel Prize in two different sciences.

Marie's birthplace in Warsaw is now a museum dedicated to Marie and her work.

Polish Upbringing

Marie Curie was born Maria Sklodowska on November 7, 1867, in Warsaw, Poland. At the time of Maria's birth, Poland was no longer a country. After a series of wars, Poland had been divided up among many countries in 1815. The Russian Empire controlled the area where Maria's family lived. But the family was still loyal to Poland. Some Poles tried to fight for independence from the Russian Empire. But it was dangerous for Maria's family and other Poles to even speak Polish.

Tragedy

For much of Maria's childhood, her mother, Bronislawa, was sick with tuberculosis. She had to leave the home for long periods of time to get treatment. In 1873 Maria's father, Wladyslaw, was fired from his job as an assistant school director because of his Polish background. Maria's father opened up his family's home as a boarding school to make money. In 1874 Maria's oldest sister Zosia became very sick. She died in 1876. Then just two years and three months later Maria's mother also passed away. Maria was only ten years old.

Schooldays

Maria's parents made education and learning priorities in their children's lives. Maria and her four siblings had mostly been home schooled. But after the tragic death of her mother and sister, Maria's father thought it would be good for her to attend public school. However, many of the teachers in public schools were anti-Polish. This made school hard for Maria. But overall, Maria enjoyed learning. She graduated first in her class in 1883. She was only 15 years old.

After graduating, Maria wanted to continue her education. However, there were few options for women in Warsaw at this time. Maria would have to study at a university in a different country, such as France, that allowed women students. But this

Forbidden Science

The Russian government, which controlled Warsaw and other areas that were once part of Poland, had strict rules about what Poles were and were not allowed to do. This way Poles would be less likely to gain power and try to take back control of the country. In addition to other restrictions, Poles were forbidden from teaching or learning laboratory science. But Maria and many others learned about science and other forbidden topics in secret.

Maria, *far left*, poses with her father, *seated*, and two surviving sisters Bronia, *middle*, and Hela, *right*, in 1890.

was expensive, and her family did not have much money. Maria's college plans would have to wait.

Maria's older sister Bronia also wanted to go to a University. However, the Russian government did not support women continuing their education beyond public school. The government believed women should care for their homes and raise their children. So Maria and Bronia met in secret with other female Warsaw scholars. They gathered in each other's homes and read books to gain knowledge. Maria soon discovered that she had a talent for understanding math, physics, and chemistry. Around this time, Maria got to work in a laboratory for the first time. It was owned by one of her cousins. Maria was able to do experiments there. But she still longed for more education.

The Flying University

While in Warsaw, Maria and Bronia met with a group of other Polish women who wanted to learn. This secret group was called the Flying University. The group did not meet at an actual building or university. Instead, students met in living rooms or at institutions that supported their cause. The Sklodowska family was involved in the Flying University since its start in 1882.

When Maria was allowed to use her cousin's laboratory, she learned about performing basic experiments. She later reflected:

I tried out various experiments described in treatises on physics and chemistry, and the results were sometimes unexpected. At times I would be encouraged by a little unhoped-for success, at others I would be in the deepest despair because of accidents and failures resulting from my inexperience. But on the whole, though I was taught that the way of progress is neither swift nor easy, this first trial confirmed in me the taste for experimental research in the fields of physics and chemistry.

Source: Marie Curie. "Secret Studies in Warsaw." Marie Curie: In Her Own Words. American Institute of Physics, n.d. Web. Accessed January 2, 2014.

What's the Big Idea?

Take a close look at this passage. What point is Maria making about experiments and science? What did she learn about herself through her experiments? Pick out details she uses to support her points.

CHAPTER TWO

A FEMALE SCIENTIST

Both Maria and Bronia still dreamed of studying at a university. But they did not have the money to go away to school. They decided to help each other. First, Maria would help Bronia pay for college by working as a governess. Then, when Bronia finished school and had a job, she would pay for Maria's college. Maria moved to

Maria worked in the Szczuki family home as a governess for three years.

a country village outside of Warsaw to work as a governess.

When Maria wasn't working, she continued to teach herself. She realized that she most enjoyed math, physics, and chemistry. By the fall of 1891, Maria finally had enough money to go to school. But new challenges awaited her.

A Student in Paris

Maria attended the University of Paris, known as the Sorbonne, in France. She went by "Marie" because it was the French form of Maria. Marie worked very hard at the university. Sometimes she was so busy with her studies that she skipped meals or didn't sleep. But Marie was delighted by all of the new things she was learning in Paris.

Looking for a Laboratory

In summer 1893, Marie earned her master's degree in physics. She was one of only two women granted the degree that year at the Sorbonne. Marie wanted to

Marie enjoyed her time studying at the Sorbonne in Paris.

continue at the Sorbonne and study math. But it cost a lot of money. Luckily, she was given a scholarship. A year later, she completed her master's degree in math.

While completing her math degree, the Society for the Encouragement of National Industry hired Marie as a scientist. They wanted her to study the magnetic properties of steel. She was able to share lab space with a professor she knew. But she hoped to find a larger space.

Marie's search for a bigger lab led her to Pierre Curie. Pierre was a friend of one of Marie's friends. Marie and Pierre both had an interest in science. They soon fell in love. They were married on July 26, 1895.

Pierre Curie

Pierre was an accomplished scientist by the time Marie met him. He and his brother Jacques studied crystals. Pierre was also well known for his research on the relationship between magnetism and temperature. Pierre deeply respected Marie's work. Sometimes people tried to credit Pierre with Marie's work. But Pierre made sure to give the credit to Marie.

Working Mother

Marie continued to research the magnetic properties of steel. She was able to use lab space at the Municipal School of

Pierre and Marie Curie pose with their bicycles in 1895 while on their honeymoon.

Industrial Physics and Chemistry, where Pierre worked as a professor.

In September 1897, the Curies had a daughter, Irene. Most mothers during this time period were expected to stay home to take care of their children. But Marie wanted to continue working. Pierre supported Marie's desire to work. He knew how important it was to her. Pierre's father helped care for Irene while Marie continued her studies. Marie then set her sights on earning a doctorate degree in science. No other woman in the world had achieved this degree at the time.

Scientist Mother

Marie approached motherhood with enthusiasm and interest. She took detailed notes on her baby Irene's development. But Marie wanted to continue devoting her time to research as well. Pierre's father had recently lost his wife. He offered to move in with the Curies and help take care of Irene. It was a wonderful solution for Marie. She was able to continue her research. And Irene and her grandfather formed a close bond.

Even after becoming a mother, Marie was still determined to further her scientific education.

CHAPTER THREE

DISCOVERING NEW ELEMENTS

I n 1895 German scientist Wilhelm Conrad Röntgen discovered X-rays. To get an X-ray image, a film is placed behind a person. X-rays are then directed at the film. The X-rays that pass through the body make it to the film on the other side. They make the black and gray parts of an X-ray image. The darker the black, the more rays are able to pass through. The white parts of an X-ray image show up when very few

Scientist Wilhelm Conrad Röntgen's discovery of X-rays paved the way for Curie's work with rays and the discovery of new elements.

X-rays are able to pass though the body. That means more of the rays are blocked by something dense, such as bones. People were fascinated by the first X-ray images. Nobody had ever seen anything like it before.

Emitting Rays

Then in 1896, another French scientist, Henri Becquerel, discovered that the element uranium also emitted a ray. Becquerel came upon this discovery when he noticed that uranium created a fog on a film when it was kept in the dark. He guessed that the fog was probably caused by rays coming from uranium. The public was less interested in this discovery. But the uranium rays caught Curie's interest. She began to study them.

Curie used a device called the Curie electrometer. Pierre and his brother had made it years earlier. It could measure very small electrical changes in the air. Curie used it to see if rays came from uranium. She used a compound called pitchblende, which contained uranium. A compound is a material that is made up of two or more elements.

After many tests, Curie confirmed Becquerel's findings. Uranium emitted rays. She started testing other elements to see if they did too. She found that thorium also emitted rays. Curie made up a new word to describe elements giving off these rays. She called it "radioactivity."

The Curie Electrometer

Much of Curie's early work would not have been possible without the use of the Curie electrometer. This instrument recorded electrical changes in the air. When uranium rays passed through the air, the electrometer recorded a tiny change in the electrical measurement of the air. No change was recorded if there was no uranium. This helped Curie show that the uranium in the pitchblende was emitting something into the air.

Twin Discoveries

Curie was determined to find out what other elements were radioactive. Pierre was so interested in Curie's new work that he decided to join her. Curie

Marie and Pierre worked together to test radioactivity and discover two new elements.

discovered that some pitchblende containing uranium was more radioactive than uranium on its own. She wondered if there were other radioactive elements in the pitchblende.

Curie had to separate the elements that made up the pitchblende. This helped her see which ones were radioactive. This was not easy. Curie had to use many different methods to remove elements from the compound. For example, she might dissolve one element away using acid. Or she would burn it away at a set temperature.

After a lot of work, Marie and Pierre discovered a new element in the pitchblende. It was more radioactive than uranium. On July 20, 1898, Curie announced the new element. She named it polonium in honor of her home country, Poland.

Harmful Rays

Some rays, such as ultraviolet rays given off by the sun, are usually harmless. But other rays can kill the cells that make up living things. These rays can be harmful to people. Curie did not know it, but both radium and polonium give off rays that can harm living tissue.

But Curie was not finished. In December 1898, she revealed yet another new element. Marie and Pierre named the new element radium. It was much

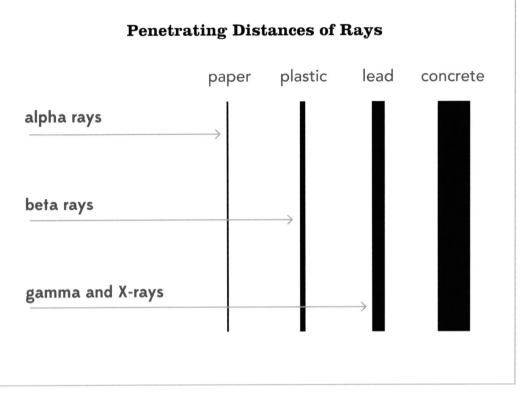

Penetrating Distances of Rays

paper   plastic   lead   concrete

alpha rays

beta rays

gamma and X-rays

Different Types of Rays

When Curie first discovered polonium and radium, she only knew that they gave off some type of ray. As more scientists became involved in measuring rays, they would discover that there are many different types of rays. This diagram shows the different types of rays and what substances they can pass through. We now know that polonium emits alpha rays, and radium emits both alpha and gamma rays. How does the chart help you better understand how rays work? Do you think beta rays could pass through human flesh?

more radioactive than uranium. As Curie was able

to isolate larger pieces of radium, she discovered

something else—they glowed!

Finding the proper space for a laboratory was often a challenge for Curie. In her autobiography, she remembered this struggle:

> The School of Physics could give us no suitable premises, but for lack of anything better, the Director permitted us to use an abandoned shed which had been in service as a dissecting room of the School of Medicine. Its glass roof did not afford complete shelter against rain; the heat was suffocating in summer, and the bitter cold of winter was only a little lessened by the iron stove, except in its immediate vicinity. There was no question of obtaining the needed proper apparatus in common use by chemists. We simply had some old pine-wood tables with furnaces and gas burners.

Source: Marie Curie. "The Struggle to Isolate Radium." Marie Curie: In Her Own Words. American Institute of Physics, n.d. Web. Accessed January 2, 2014.

Nice View

After reading this passage from Curie's autobiography, go back and read Chapter Three again. How does Curie's description of her laboratory make you think differently about her accomplishments? Write a short paragraph about how this quote changes your ideas about Curie's work.

CHAPTER FOUR

A NOBEL PRIZE

The discovery of two new elements was a huge achievement. But Curie did not stop there. She made another major discovery. Curie realized that no matter how she heated or cooled a radioactive element, it still gave off the same level of radioactivity. It did not matter if the element was solid, powdered, or in a gas form. It did not matter what the temperature of the element

After discovering polonium and radium, Curie continued to research and experiment with radioactivity.

was either. It always emitted the same level of radioactivity.

Curie guessed that the radioactivity was not caused by a chemical reaction. A chemical reaction happens when the atoms that make up different elements react to one another. Instead, Curie believed radioactivity was an atomic property of the radioactive element. That meant the radioactivity was built into the atoms that made up the element.

In the years to come, scientists would reveal that Curie's hypothesis was correct. But at the time, Curie was not interested in proving her theory. Instead, she focused on learning more about the new elements. She wanted to study how they might help people.

Strange Illnesses

Curie found that polonium was hard to collect in large amounts. So she worked with Pierre on new ways to isolate radium. But their health suffered. It was not yet known that radioactive materials could hurt people. Pierre often had intense attacks of pain. Curie lost

20 pounds (9 kg). And they both suffered burns and sores on their fingers from handling the radioactive elements. But neither believed that it was their research that was making them sick.

Academic Success

Despite these illnesses, Curie continued with her research. In June 1903, she became the first woman in France to earn a doctorate degree. It was a huge achievement.

In December 1903, Marie and Pierre were awarded the Nobel Prize in Physics for their research on radioactivity. This was the first time in history that

The Dangers of Radiation

Both Marie and Pierre suffered from mysterious illnesses that were likely a result of being around radioactive elements so often. Radiation can damage the human body. It can cause nausea, hair loss, and tiredness. Large amounts of radiation can cause burns on human skin. Radiation can also cause cancer. When radiation damages the cells that make up a person's body, the body tries to repair the damage. But sometimes the repair process can result in the body producing cancerous cells.

Curie sits with her two daughters Eve, *left*, and Irene, *right*.

a woman received a Nobel Prize. Pierre was careful to give Marie full credit for her research. But many people thought women could not be good scientists. Some thought that Pierre had done most of the work. Curie did her best to ignore the criticisms and focus on her work. Marie and Pierre's work became more popular after they won the Nobel Prize. The press hounded them for information about their personal lives and their discoveries.

Tragedy

In December 1904, Curie gave birth to another daughter, Eve. But tragedy soon struck the family. In April 1906, Pierre was struck by a horse-drawn wagon while crossing the street. He died instantly. Curie was devastated. But she knew she must continue her work. The Sorbonne hired Curie to take over Pierre's position as a professor. This made her the first female professor at the Sorbonne. She continued her work, trying to discover more radioactive elements.

EXPLORE ONLINE

The website below has even more information about Marie and Pierre Curie's discovery of polonium and radium. As you know, every source is different. Reread Chapter Four of this book. What are the similarities between Chapter Four and the information you found on the website? Are there any differences? How do the two sources present information differently?

Discovery of Polonium and Radium
www.mycorelibrary.com/marie-curie

FOR THE COMMON GOOD

Curie had been popular in the media for most of her career. But soon the press turned on her. After Pierre's death, Curie had a relationship with a married man who used to be Pierre's student. In 1911 the media published news of the affair. Curie and her daughters met swarms of the press wherever they went. Around the same time, Curie offered herself as a candidate for a seat at the

The press snapped a photo of Curie, middle right, with her daughters Irene, middle left, Eve, right, and friend Mrs. Meloney, left, arriving in New York on the ship Olympic.

French Academy of Sciences. She did not get it. Some believe this may have been in part because of the news about her in the media.

In the midst of the scandal, Curie received good news. She was awarded a second Nobel Prize. This time the prize was in the field of chemistry. It was for the discovery of radium and polonium and how it impacted the understanding of radioactivity. This was the first time in history that someone had won two Nobel Prizes. Curie now had a Nobel Prize in physics and in chemistry.

But the scandal had deeply affected Curie. She and her daughters did their best to stay out of the public eye. They traveled away from Paris. In January 1912, Curie was in the hospital for kidney problems. She also suffered from depression. In March Curie underwent an operation on her kidneys. It left her very weak. By October 1912, the scandal had mostly blown over. Curie and her family returned to Paris. In

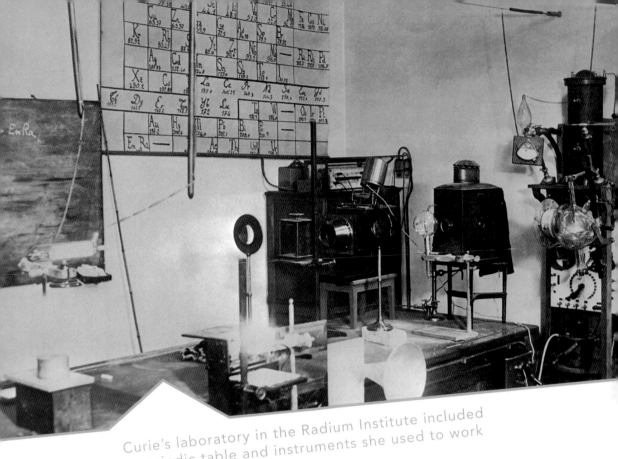

Curie's laboratory in the Radium Institute included a periodic table and instruments she used to work with radium.

December 1912, she finally felt well enough to return to her research.

The Radium Institute

With the scandal over, Curie wanted to do something to honor Pierre. So she helped create the Radium Institute, which would focus on radium research. Curie was put in charge of the radioactivity laboratory.

The building was completed in July 1914. Before Curie could start working in the lab, World War I (1914–1918) began. Most of Curie's researchers went to fight for France.

The War Effort

Curie wanted to do something to help the war effort. She knew that X-ray equipment could help doctors treat wounded soldiers. This technology could save lives. Curie convinced the French government to help her set up these services for soldiers. She was named director of the Red Cross Radiology Service.

As director, Curie set up cars that could transport X-ray equipment wherever it was needed. Curie knew little about

Radiation for Treating Cancer

Today, radiation is used to treat some types of cancer. Radiation can damage cancer cells by shrinking them or keeping them from growing. Doctors can give radiation treatment through medicine, rays from outside the body, and small implants that release radiation at the site of the cancer.

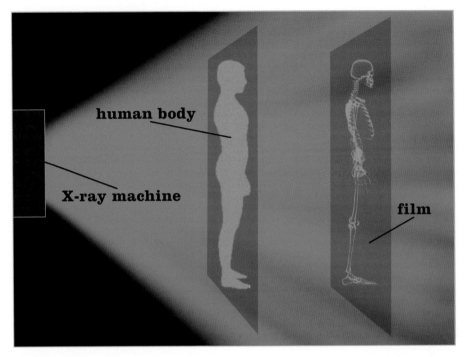

X-Ray Machine

The image above shows how an X-ray machine works. The bones in the body stop most of the X-rays, but some X-rays get through. The X-rays that make it through land on a film, making an image of the body's bones. How does this picture help you better understand X-rays? Is there anything that surprises you about the picture?

X-ray technology, so she taught herself. Her 17-year-old daughter, Irene, became her assistant. Curie also taught other women about X-ray technology at the Radium Institute.

Curie hoped radium could also help wounded soldiers. In 1915 she collected radon, a gas that comes from radium. Doctors could apply the radon where a patient had diseased tissue from a wound. The radiation was supposed to help heal the wound. But it was not always successful.

Final Days

World War I ended on November 11, 1918. Curie went back to focusing on the Radium Institute. In 1920 she created the Curie Foundation to help fund the Radium Institute. The foundation later became focused on treating cancer.

But Curie began feeling sick again. Some people were starting to notice the harmful effects of radiation. Curie was still convinced that it was not dangerous. In May

Leaving Radiation Behind

Even though Curie conducted her experiments almost 100 years ago, her papers, equipment, and even the furniture in her lab are still radioactive. Her laboratory in Paris was decontaminated using special chemicals. But everything inside was removed. If anyone wants to view her documents, they must wear protective clothing.

1934, she left the lab early, feeling sick. She was never well enough to return. None of Curie's doctors could figure out what caused her sickness. Curie died on July 4, 1934.

Marie Curie will long be remembered for her amazing contributions to science. Because of her, the benefits and the dangers of radiation are understood much better. She also paved the way for the equality of women in the science field and beyond.

FURTHER EVIDENCE

Chapter Five discusses Curie's final days and death. What is one of the chapter's main points? What evidence supports this point? Take a look at the website below. Does the information on the website support the information in this chapter? Write a few sentences in support of this chapter's main point based on information you find on the website.

Marie Curie's Obituary
www.mycorelibrary.com/marie-curie

Polonium

Marie Curie discovered the element polonium. Because it is radioactive, polonium is very toxic. But it has served a great purpose in space. Polonium generates a lot of heat even in small amounts. So it can be used to power satellites in space, which need to be lightweight. Someday, polonium may also help power spacecraft.

Radioactivity

Curie was one of the first scientists to recognize and study radioactivity. Today, radioactive substances are used in medical devices, in manufacturing, and even to produce energy. Radioactive substances are used in our everyday lives. For example, most smoke detectors use a radioactive source to sense smoke in the air. Radiation is also commonly used to treat various types of cancer.

Radium

Curie had high hopes that radium could be used to help people suffering from various ailments. The gas that radium produces, called radon, has had success in treating some types of cancer. However, today it is generally considered too dangerous due to its radioactivity.

Say What?

Reading about radioactivity and the discovery of elements can mean learning a lot of new vocabulary. Find five words in this book that you have never heard or seen before. Use a dictionary to find out what they mean. Then write the meanings in your own words and use each word in a new sentence.

Surprise Me

Chapter One gives information about Curie's childhood. She lived in a very different time and place than you do. She dealt with many challenges. What was most surprising about Curie's childhood? What did you learn from Chapter One that was new to you? Write a few sentences about what you learned.

Why Do I Care?

Marie Curie did her research more than 100 years ago. But that doesn't mean her work isn't relevant today. How do Curie's discoveries affect your life? How might your life be different if Curie had not discovered radioactivity?

You Are There

Imagine you are a scientist working in your lab and you hear about radioactivity for the first time. What questions do you have for Curie and other scientists studying this new discovery? How do you feel about Curie's discovery of new radioactive elements?

GLOSSARY

acid
a chemical substance that can dissolve some elements

atom
small pieces that join together to make an element

dissolve
to become mixed in with a liquid

doctorate degree
the highest degree obtainable in graduate school

element
a chemical substance that cannot be broken down

emit
to give off

governess
a woman employed as a teacher for children at a private home

hypothesis
an educated guess often made and tested by scientists

isolate
to separate something so it is alone

scandal
an immoral act that shocks people and disgraces the people involved

scholarship
a sum of money given to a student to help pay for his or her education

LEARN MORE

Books

Borzendowski, Janice. *Marie Curie: Mother of Modern Physics*. New York: Sterling, 2009.

Cobb, Vicki. *Marie Curie*. New York: DK Publishing, 2008.

Lin, Yoming S. *The Curies and Radioactivity*. New York: PowerKids Press, 2012.

Websites

To learn more about Great Minds of Science, visit **booklinks.abdopublishing.com**. These links are routinely monitored and updated to provide the most current information available.

Visit **www.mycorelibrary.com** for free additional tools for teachers and students.

INDEX

ABOUT THE AUTHOR

Katherine Krieg is the author of more than 20 books for young readers. She is an advocate for science education.